It's Due When ?!?

Written and Illustrated by
B. K. Hixson

It's Due When ?!?

A Practical Remedy for the
Annual science Fair Panic Attack

Copyright © 2001
First Printing • June 2001
B. K. Hixson

Published by Loose in the Lab, Inc.
9462 South 560 West
Sandy, Utah 84070

www.looseinthelab.com

Library of Congress Cataloging-in-Publication Data:

Hixson, B. K., 1957-
    It's Due When?!?/B. K. Hixson
    p.   cm.-(Loose in the Lab Science Series)

    Includes index
    ISBN 0-9660965-8-4
  1. Science Projects methodology. [1. Science Fair Ideas-
methodology 2. Experiments] I. B. K. Hixson III. Loose
in the Lab IV. Title V. Series
Q182.3 B79 2001
507.8-dc21

Printed in the United States of America
Land of Innovation & Invention!

Dedication

For Dee Strange
(the short one)

My good friend and colleague from Hermosa Valley School, whose room is a giant ongoing science fair project. This is for all the trips to the desert to drink date shakes, steal exotic varieties of kumquats, and share bright pink beavertail cactus blossoms with the fifth graders. It's for all the wonderful sights that appear when you don a diving mask and disappear under the water at CIMI on Catalina Island with the seventh graders, and for the hundreds of science fair projects we reviewed every year. Thank you so much for inviting me to be a part of the staff!

Onward, Forward!

Acknowledgments

There are always a lot of thank-yous that need to be passed out when a book gets published, and this one is no exception. At the top of the list are all the kids who have passed through my classroom and have patiently waded through my meanderings, expectations, and occasional apologies for heaping upon them the weight of the universe. So, kids of Fowler Junior High and Hermosa Valley School, thank you and hopefully, now that some of you are parents, the fruit of your hard work will benefit your own kids.

As for my educational outlook, the hands-on perspective, and the use of humor in the classroom, Dr. Fox, my senior professor at Oregon State University, gets the credit for shaping my educational philosophy while simultaneously recognizing that even at the collegiate level we were on to something a little different. He did his very best to encourage, nurture, and support me while I was getting basketloads of opposition for being willing to swim upstream. There were also several colleagues who did their very best to channel my enthusiasm during those early, formative years of teaching: Dick Bishop, Dick Hinton, Dee Strange, and Linda Zimmermann. Thanks for your patience, friendship, and support.

Next up are all the folks that get to do the dirty work that make the final publication look so polished but very rarely get the credit they deserve. Our resident graphics gurus, Ed Seghini and Ben Francom each get a nod for scanning and cleaning the artwork you find on these pages, as well as putting together the graphics that make up the cover. A warm Yankee yahoo to Sue Moore our editor who passes her comments on so that Kathleen Hixson, Diane Burns, and Sue Moore (once again) can take turns simultaneously proofreading the text while mocking my writing skills.

Once we have a finished product, it has to be printed by the good folks at Advanced Graphics—Michael Williams, Matt and the crew—so that Stefan Kohler, Louisa Walker, Kent Walker, and the Delta Education gang can market and ship the books, collect the money, and send us a couple of nickels. It's a short thank-you for a couple of very important jobs.

Mom and Dad, as always, get the end credits. Thanks for the education, encouragement, and love. And for Kathy and the kids—Porter, Shelby, Courtney, and Aubrey—hugs and kisses.

Reproduction Rights

There is very little about this book that is truly formal, but at the insistence of our wise and esteemed counsel, let us declare: *No part of this book may be reproduced or utilized in any form or by any means, electronic or mechanical, including photocopying, recording, or by any information storage and retrieval system, without permission in writing from the publisher.* That would be us.

More Legal Stuff

If, for some reason, perhaps even beyond your own control, you have an affinity for disaster, we wish you well. *But we, in no way, take any responsibility for any injury that is incurred to any person using the information provided in this book or for any damage to personal property or effects that are directly or indirectly a result of the suggested activities contained herein.* Translation: You're on your own. Make sure you have a clear path to the door if it starts to smoke.

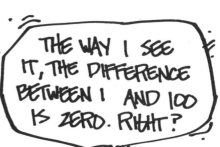

THE WAY I SEE IT, THE DIFFERENCE BETWEEN 1 AND 100 IS ZERO. RIGHT?

Table of Contents

Introduction

Step 1 • The Hypothesis

Step 2 • Gather Information

Step 3 • Design Your Experiment

Step 4 • Conduct the Experiment

Step 5 • Gathering & Evaluating the Data

Step 6 • Present Your Ideas

About This Book

The Scientific Method

Moms, dads, and kids will find that the experience and end product are of a higher quality if they all work together. We are writing this book with the assumption that the majority of the work will be completed by the student, but, this is a learning process and a little over-the-shoulder supervision is recommended.

There are generally six steps to completing a science fair project. We have created an icon, a piece of art, to associate with each step. A description of the process and the icons we are going to use are found in the following order:

1. Generate a Hypothesis

The first step of the process is to take an experiment that you are familiar with and change one of the variables. Based on your experience make a prediction, or hypothesis, about what you think the outcome of the experiment with the new variable will most likely be.

2. Gather Background Information

Read about your topic. Define words that are particular to your idea, explain concepts that relate, and, if possible, provide some historical perspective by either charting and explaining the development of the idea or chronicling the accomplishments of some of the more famous scientists that preceded you.

Use books, magazines, people, the Internet, encyclopedias, and textbooks, anything that will help you develop a strong understanding of your idea.

3. Design an Experiment

List the materials you will need, consider safety needs, create a lab procedure, generate data tables. Have an adult approve the process before you actually begin to experiment.

4. Perform the Experiment

This is game time, to use a sports metaphor. Time to put all your studying and planning to work. You will want to not only do the experiment, but also repeat it at least twice and, if possible, three times to get a good sample of data. Which leads us to our next section.

5. Collect & Record Experimental Data

Record the data, take pictures, make drawings, construct graphs and use them to explain and interpret your information.

You are going to want to be able to use your data to explain your hypothesis, create models to support it, draw conclusions from it, and generally either support or refute your initial idea.

6. Present Your Findings

You will want to write up your science fair project. Use the checklist that we have provided in this book on page 91. You may also be asked to give an oral presentation; check page 102. And finally, most science fair projects must be displayed. We have the definitive checklists that will get you to the top of the pig pile.

National Standards

The National Research Council produced the National Education Standards as a guideline for educators to refer to when developing their science programs. Under the heading *Science as Inquiry*, we find the following objectives.

The National Content Standards (Grades K-4)

1. *Ask a question about objects, organisms, and events in the environment.*
2. *Plan and conduct a simple investigation.*
3. *Employ simple equipment and tools to gather data and extend the senses.*
4. *Use data to construct a reasonable explanation.*
5. *Communicate investigations and explanations.*

The National Content Standards (Grades 5-8)

1. *Identify questions that can be answered through scientific investigations.*
2. *Design and conduct a scientific investigation.*
3. *Use appropriate tools and techniques to gather, analyze, and interpret data.*
4. *Develop descriptions, explanations, predictions, and models using evidence.*
5. *Think critically and logically to make the relationships between evidence and explanations.*
6. *Recognize and analyze alternative explanations and predictions.*
7. *Communicate scientific procedures and explanations.*
8. *Use mathematics in all aspects of scientific inquiry.*

These standards are thoroughly covered in the six chapters we have developed to help you create a successful science fair project, including the written report and the oral presentation. Bureaucrats of the world rejoice!

And, Why So Silly?

A word about humor. Science is not usually known for being funny, even though Bill Nye of *The Science Guy*, Beaker from *Sesame Street*, and *Beakman's World* do their best to mingle the two. That's all fine and dandy, but we want you to know that we incorporate humor because it is scientifically (and educationally) sound to do so. Plus, it's really at the root of our personalities. Here's what we know:

When we laugh . . .

a. Pupils dilate, increasing the amount of light entering the eye.

b. Our heart rate increases, pumping more blood to the brain.

c. Oxygen-rich blood to the brain means the brain is able to collect, process, and store more information, which leads to increased comprehension.

d. Laughter relaxes muscles, which can be involuntarily tense if a student is uncomfortable or fearful of an academic topic.

e. Laughter stimulates the immune system, which will ultimately translate into overall health and fewer kids who say they are sick of science.

f. Socially, it provides an acceptable pause in the academic routine, which then gives the student time to regroup and prepare to address some of the more difficult ideas with a renewed spirit. They can study longer and focus on ideas more efficiently.

g. Laughter releases chemicals in the brain that are associated with pleasure and joy.

And Now,
Your Guide ...

Science Fair Projects

As simple as science fair project versus science reports sounds, it gets screwed up millions of times a year by sweet, unsuspecting students who are counseled by sweet, unknowing, and probably just as confused parents.

To give you a sense of contrast, we have provided a list of legitimate science fair projects and then reports that do not qualify. We will also add some comments in italics that should help clarify why they do or do not qualify in the science fair project department.

Science Fair Projects

1. Temperature and the amount of time it takes mealworms to change to beetles.

Great start. We have chosen a single variable that is easy to measure: temperature. From this point forward the student can read, explore, and formulate an original question that is the foundation for the project.

A colleague of mine actually did a similar type of experiment for his master's degree. His topic: The rate of development of fly larvae in cow poop as a function of temperature. No kidding. He found out that the warmer the temperature of the poop, the faster the larvae developed into flies.

2. The effect of different concentrations of soapy water on seed germination.

Again, wonderful. Measuring the concentration of soapy water. This leads naturally into lots of opportunities to generate original questions and a good project. Be sure to isolate a single variable and not try to test several things at once.

vs. Science Reports

3. Crystal size and the amount of sugar in the solution.
This could lead into other factors such as exploring the temperature of the solution, the size of the solution container, and other variables that may affect crystal growth. Opens a lot of doors.

4. Helicopter rotor size and the speed at which it falls.
Size also means surface area, which is very easy to measure. The student who did this not only found the mathematical threshold with relationship to air friction, but she had a ton of fun.

5. The ideal ratio of baking soda to vinegar to make a fire extinguisher.
Another great start. Easy to measure and track, leads to a logical question that can either be supported or refuted with the data.

6. The relationship between the length of an instrument and the pitch that it produces.
There are lots of ways to go. The length, the diameter, and the kind of material are all possibilities.

Each of those topics *measures* one thing, such as the amount of sugar, the concentration of soapy water, or the ideal size. If you start with an idea that allows you to measure something, then you can change it, ask questions, explore, and ultimately make a *prediction*, also called a *hypothesis*, and experiment to find out if you are correct.

Science Reports

1. Dinosaurs!

OK, great. Everyone loves dinosaurs, but where is the experiment? Did you find a new dinosaur? Is Jurassic Park alive and well, and we are headed there to breed, drug, or in some way test them? Probably not. This was a report on T. rex. Cool, but not a science fair project.

2. Our Friend the Sun

Another very large topic, no pun intended. This could be a great topic. Sunlight is fascinating. It can be split, polarized, reflected, refracted, measured, collected, converted. However, this poor kid simply chose to write about the size of the sun and regurgitate facts about its features, cycles, and other astrofacts while simultaneously offending the American Melanoma Survivors Society. Just kidding about that last part.

3. Smokers' Poll

A lot of folks think they are headed in the right direction here. Again, it depends on how the kid attacks the idea. Are they going to single out race? Heredity? Shoe size? What exactly are they after here? The young lady who did this report chose to make it more of a psychology-studies effort than a scientific report.

4. The Majestic Moose

If you went out and caught the moose, drugged it to see the side effects for disease control, or even mated it with an elk to determine if you could create an animal that would become the spokesanimal for the Alabama Dairy Farmers' Got Melk? promotion, that would be fine. But, another fact-filled report should be filed with the English teacher.

5. How Tadpoles Change into Frogs

Great start, but they forgot to finish the statement. We know how tadpoles change into frogs. What we don't know is how tadpoles change into frogs if they are in an altered environment, if they are hatched out of cycle, if they are stuck under the tire of an off-road vehicle blatantly driving through a protected wetland area. That's what we want to know. How tadpoles change into frogs, if, when, or under what measurable circumstances.

One Final Comment

Quite often I discuss the scientific method with moms, dads, teachers, and kids, and get the impression that, according to their understanding, there is one, and only one, scientific method. This is not necessarily true. There are lots of ways to investigate the world we live in and on.

Paleontologists dig up dead animals and plants but have no way to conduct experiments on them. They're dead. Albert Einstein, the most famous scientist of the last century and probably on everybody's starting five of all time, never did experiments. He was a theoretical physicist, which means that he came up with a hypothesis, skipped over collecting materials for things like black holes and space-time continuums, didn't experiment on anything or even collect data. He just went straight from hypothesis to conclusion, and he's still considered part of the scientific community. You'll probably follow the six steps we outlined but keep an open mind.

HEY!
GOOD NEWS AL,
YOU'RE STILL IN
THE CLUB.

Project Planner

This outline is designed to give you a specific set of time lines to follow as you develop your science fair project. Most teachers will give you 8 to 11 weeks notice for this kind of assignment. We are going to operate from the shorter time line with our suggested schedule, which means that the first thing you need to do is get a calendar.

A. The suggested time to be devoted to each item is listed in parentheses next to that item. Enter the date of the Science Fair and then, using the calendar, work backward entering dates.

B. As you complete each item, enter the date that you completed it in the column between the goal (due date) and project item.

Goal Completed   Project Item

1. Generate a Hypothesis (2 weeks)

_____	_____	Review Idea Section
_____	_____	Select a Topic and Several Ideas
_____	_____	Try Several Experiments
_____	_____	Narrow Ideas to Single Experiment
_____	_____	Hypothesis Generated
_____	_____	Finished Hypothesis Submitted
_____	_____	Hypothesis Approved

2. Gather Background Information (1 week)

_____	_____	Concepts/Discoveries Written Up
_____	_____	Vocabulary/Glossary Completed
_____	_____	Famous Scientists in Field

Goals, & Time Line

Goal Completed   Project Item

3. Design an Experiment (1 week)

_____	_____	Procedure Written
_____	_____	Lab Safety Review Completed
_____	_____	Procedure Approved
_____	_____	Data Tables Prepared & Approved
_____	_____	Materials List Completed
_____	_____	Materials Acquired

4. Perform the Experiment (2 weeks)

_____	_____	Scheduled Lab Time
_____	_____	Lab Activity Repeated
_____	_____	Lab Activity Checked a Third Time

5. Collect and Record Experimental Data (part of 4)

_____	_____	Data Tables Completed
_____	_____	Graphs Completed
_____	_____	Other Data Collected and Prepared

6. Present Your Findings (2 weeks)

_____	_____	Rough Draft of Paper Completed
_____	_____	Proofreading 1 Completed
_____	_____	Proofreading 2 Completed
_____	_____	Final Report Completed
_____	_____	Display Designed & Approved
_____	_____	Display Completed
_____	_____	Oral Report Outlined on Index Cards
_____	_____	Practice Presentation of Oral Report
_____	_____	Oral Report Presentation
_____	_____	Science Fair Setup
_____	_____	Show Time!

Scientific Method
• Step 1 •
The Hypothesis

"The best way to get a good idea is to get a lot of ideas."

> • Roger von Oech
> Creativity Consultant

Objectives of This Section

If you had to pick one section to be more important than the others, this would be it. A good hypothesis will guide and direct everything you do to the conclusion of the project. Take the time to create an original hypothesis that can be tested with a single variable, and you are well on your way to a successful experience.

____ 1. Pick a general topic in science, like physics or botany, that is interesting to you and that you want to study.

____ 2. Find an experiment in that field that gives you lots of options when it comes time to adapt it for your project.

____ 3. Bend, fold, spindle, and mutilate the variables of the experiment to produce a new lab idea—something that has not been explored yet.

____ 4. Select one idea that you want to tinker with and write it as a statement, or an educated guess that contains only one variable. Check the hypothesis you have written by asking two simple questions: 1) Did I make a prediction? and 2) Can my prediction be measured and evaluated using an experiment?

Marketing 101

Three very successful and equally competitive businessmen owned shops in a downtown area right next door to each other. In an effort to boost sales and outdo his rivals, the shop owner to the east made a very large sign with bright red letters that said, "Year End Close Out Sale! 40% Off Everything!"

Upon his arrival the next morning, the owner to the west noticed the sign and retired to his shop, only to emerge a few minutes later with an equally large, red lettered sign that read, "Going Out of Business Sale! Everything 50% Off! Today Only!"

When the fella who owned the middle shop showed up, he casually took note of his competitors' ambitions and went inside his store. A few minutes later he emerged with his own sign, somewhat smaller, that he placed over his door. It read, "Main Entrance."

Be adaptable in your thinking.

Brain Tickler #1

Kids that create successful science fair projects take a peek at what is out there and then tweak it just a bit. Sometimes it doesn't take very much to give you a really great, new idea.

Before you decide it would be easier to suck a pregnant rhinoceros through a straw than come up with an original science fair idea, try out this brain tickler. Sometimes the solution is right in front of your eyes but you're looking too hard to see it right away.

Here's Your Assignment: Review the following sequence of letters. Your task is to cross out *six letters* so that the remaining letters, keeping the sequence exactly the same, spell a very common word. We've included a couple of practice lines if you don't get it on the first try. The answer is given in the back of the book, but resist the temptation to flip back there right away. Take a couple to the chin.

BSAINXLEATNTEARS

BSAINXLEATNTEARS   BSAINXLEATNTEARS

BSAINXLEATNTEARS   BSAINXLEATNTEARS

BSAINXLEATNTEARS   BSAINXLEATNTEARS

BSAINXLEATNTEARS   BSAINXLEATNTEARS

BSAINXLEATNTEARS   BSAINXLEATNTEARS

BSAINXLEATNTEARS   BSAINXLEATNTEARS

Brain Tickler #2

Sometimes great ideas are right in front of your face and it drives you bananas until you figure it out. Sorry, couldn't resist. Other times you can solve a problem if you remove artificial boundaries that don't even exist. If you're thinking, "Brain Tickler, Round 2," you're right.

"The second assault on the same problem should come from a totally different direction."

- Tom Hirshfield
  Physicist

Here's Your Assignment: Pictured below is a pattern of nine dots arranged in a symmetrical pattern. Connect all of the dots using no more than four straight lines. The only rules are that you may not rearrange the dots and you may not lift your pen or pencil off the page. Good luck.

Again, we have given you a couple of extra patterns on the next page to work with if you happen to miss the mark the first time out. The answer is, again, on page 110, for those of you afraid to stretch yourself a bit and go out of bounds to solve the problem . . . I'm not sure, but that could have been a hint.

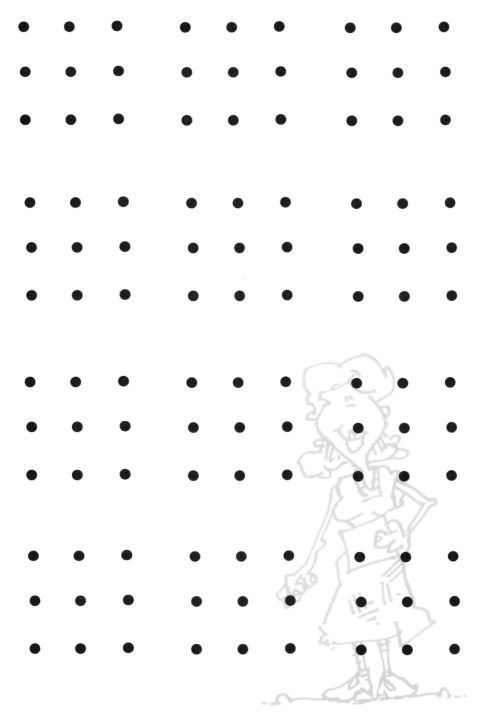

Generating Your Hypothesis

A hypothesis is an educated guess. It is a statement of what you think will probably happen based on some experience. It is also the most important part of your science fair project because it directs the entire process. It determines what you study, the materials you need, and how the experiment is designed, carried out, and evaluated. Needless to say, you need to put some thought into this part.

There are four steps to generating a hypothesis:

Step One • Pick a Topic

Preferably something that you are interested in studying. We would like to politely recommend that you take a peek at physical science ideas (physics and chemistry) if you are a rookie and this is one of your first shots at a science fair project. These kinds of lab ideas allow you to repeat the experiments quickly. There is a lot of data that can be collected, and there is a huge variety to choose from.

If you are having trouble finding an idea, all you have to do is pick up a compilation of science activities and start thumbing through it. Go to the local library or head to a bookstore and you will find a wide and ever-changing selection to choose from. Find a topic that interests you and start reading. At some point an idea will catch your eye, and you will be off to the races.

Quick Check • Interests

Listed below are all of the major topics of science except theoretical physics and quantum mechanics. This is just a teaser list to help get you get focused and think of things you might otherwise overlook. Feel free to revisit this list as often as you like until you find something that tickles your fancy. When you get it narrowed down to that point, head to the library and see what books are available in that general category.

1. I like to study things that are (check one):
   ___ A. in a lab (Go to 2, Physical Science)
   ___ B. outdoors (Go to 3, Earth Science)
   ___ C. living (Go to 4, Life Science)

2. Physical Science, my interests include:
   ___ A. Mixing Chemicals
   ___ B. Building Electrical Things
   ___ C. Rockets, Planes, Balloons, Flight
   ___ D. Magnets, Magnetic Fields
   ___ E. Thermometers, Heating & Cooling Stuff
   ___ F. Light, Colors, Filters, Illusions
   ___ G. Sound, Pitch, Vibrations
   ___ H. Electronics Widgets

3. Earth Science, my interests include:
   ___ A. Rocks, Minerals, Fossils, Soil
   ___ B. Oceans and Associated Life
   ___ C. Stars, Planets, Space
   ___ D. Weather, Forecasting, Tornados

4. Life Science, my interests include:
   ___ A. Growing and Experimenting with Plants
   ___ B. Animals and Their Characteristics
   ___ C. The Human Body and How it Works
   ___ D. Microbes, Fungi, Mold, Gooey Stuff
   ___ E. Ecosystems: Forests, Swamps, Savannas

step Two • Do the Lab

Choose a lab activity that looks interesting in that field of study and try the experiment. Some kids make the mistake of thinking that all you have to do is find a lab in a book, repeat the lab, and you are on the gravy train with biscuit wheels. Your goal is to ask an ORIGINAL question, not repeat an experiment that has been done a bazillion times before.

As you do the lab, be thinking not only about the data you are collecting, but also of ways you could adapt or change the experiment to find out new information. The point of the science fair project is to have you become an actual scientist and contribute a little bit of new knowledge to the world.

You know that they don't pay all of those engineers good money to sit around and repeat other people's lab work. The company wants new ideas, so if you are able to generate and explore new ideas you become very valuable, not only to that company but to society. It is the question-askers that find cures for diseases, create new materials, figure out ways to make existing machines energy efficient, and change the way we live. For the purpose of illustration, we are going to do a lab in this book and run it through the rest of the process. The lab uses a sheet of paper, a cup of water and a pair of scissors. Cool. Easy to do. Not expensive at all and open to all kinds of adaptations, including the examples we give you as well as the ideas that you are going to come up with on your own.

Invisible Water Magnets

This introductory lab is great because it gives you all kinds of opportunities to expand the original idea. You will take a long, skinny, piece of paper and fold it into an accordion shape like the illustration below. The bottom fold on the paper is wetted and then removed from the water. The whole accordion is lowered toward the water, wet end first. Watch very closely. As the paper nears the water, a very interesting phenomenon occurs.

Materials
1   sheet of paper
1   pair of scissors
1   cup of water

Procedure
1. Cut a strip of paper from the edge of the sheet. It should be about 1 inch wide and 11 inches long.

2. Fold the paper into an accordion shape; use the illustration to the right. The folds should be about an inch apart with the last fold sticking straight down.

3. Lower the last fold to the surface of the water and get it wet. Remove the accordion from the water.

4. Now, a second time, very slowly lower it to the surface again. *Do not put it all the way in the water.* As you get closer and closer, you will notice a very interesting and unexpected response.

How Come, Huh?

To understand why the paper jumped down into the water, it is important to know what a water molecule looks like and how it behaves. Water molecules are naturally attracted to each other. As you can see, they have a positive end and a negative end, just like a magnet. The little atoms on the top that look like Mickey Mouse ears have a positive charge, or act like the north end of a magnet, and the big atom at the bottom has a negative charge and acts like the south end of a magnet. Check out the illustration below. Because they have this shape, the water molecules all line up and hang on to each other magnetically when they get close.

When the end of the paper is dipped into the water, the water molecules all line up inside the paper. As the paper is lowered to the surface of the water, the water starts to feel the pull of the water molecules in the paper. When the paper gets close enough, the water molecules in the cup tug on the water molecules in the paper magnetically and pull them down into the water to be with their other water molecule buddies.

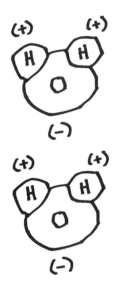

Extensions

Now the fun part. Work through the activity on the next page to take this idea and modify it into something new and original that you can explore.

Identify the Variables

Step Three • Bend, Fold, Spindle, & Mutilate Your Lab

Hopefully, you were surprised and pleased with the reaction between the wet paper and the water. Once you have picked out an experiment for your science fair project and tried it, the next thing you want to do is identify the variable in the experiment. This is because if you are going to create a new, original experiment, you will be changing the variables. In order to change them you have to be able to identify them.

The variables are the nouns of the lab sentence. In the case of the Invisible Water Magnet lab the two variables are:

1. The **liquid** (water) that was in the cup
2. The **material** (paper) that was folded and dipped

Once you have the variables identified, you can adapt and change the things that you can do to them. For example:

1. The **liquid** (water) that was in the cup
    a. Change the liquid to something new.
    b. Change the temperature of the liquid, up or down.
    c. Add something to the water.
        i. salt
        ii. electricity
2. The **material** (paper) that was folded and dipped
    a. Change the material that was dipped.
    b. Change the shape of the paper.

The key is to modify your lab into an original experiment. You want to change the experiment to make it more interesting. So. . .

Heat it	Freeze it	Reverse it	Double it
Bend it	Invert it	Poison it	Dehydrate it
Drown it	Stretch it	Fold it	Ignite it
Split it	Irradiate it	Oxidize it	Reduce it
Chill it	Speed it up	Color it	Grease it
Expand it	Substitute it	Remove it	Slow it down

Water Magnet Ideas

OK, your turn.

The variables are the nouns of the lab sentence. In the case of the Invisible Water Magnet lab the *two* variables are listed below. Your job is to fill in the blanks.

1. The **liquid** (water) that was in the cup
    a. Change the liquid to something new.
        i. _____.
        ii. _____.
        iii. _____.

    b. Change the temperature of the liquid, up or down.
    c. Add something to the water.
        i. salt
        ii. electricity
        iii. _____.

2. The **material** (paper) that was folded and dipped
    a. Change the material that was dipped.
        i. _____.
        ii. _____.
        iii. _____.

    b. Change the shape of the paper.

        i. _____.
        ii. _____.
        iii. _____.

3. Now, pick one idea from the list above and write a sentence describing your new experiment: _____

_____

_____

_____.

Sample Hypothesis Work Sheet

On the following two pages is a work sheet that will help you develop your thoughts and a hypothesis. Here is sample of the finished product to help you understand how to use it.

A. Write down the lab idea that you want to mutilate.
A mirror is placed in a tub of water. A beam of light is focused through the water onto the mirror, producing a rainbow on the wall.

B. List the possible variables you could change in the lab.
    i. **Source of light**
    ii. **The liquid in the tub**
    iii. **The distance from flashlight to mirror**

C. Take one variable listed in section B and apply one of the 24 changes to it. Write that change down and state your new lab idea in the space below.

The shape of the beam of light can be controlled by making and placing cardboard filters over the end of the flashlight. Various shapes such as circles, squares, and slits will produce different quality rainbows.

D. State your hypothesis in the space below. List the variable. Be sure that when you write the hypothesis you are making an educated guess and <u>not asking a question.</u>

Hypothesis: The narrower the beam of light the tighter, brighter, and more focused the reflected rainbow will appear.

Variable tested: **The opening on the filter**

Once you have the hypothesis in place, everything else should fall in line. You know what kind of research to do, how to set up your experiment, and the data you need to support your conclusion. Saddle up; you're ready to ride out.

Hypothesis Work Sheet

Step Three • Bend, Fold, Spindle, Work Sheet

This work sheet will give you an opportunity to work through the process of creating an original idea.

    A. Write down the lab idea that you want to mangle.

_____

_____

_____

    B. List the possible variables you could change in the lab.

        i. _____

        ii. _____

        iii. _____

        iv. _____

        v. _____

    C. Take one variable listed in section B and apply one of the 24 changes below to it. Write that change down and state your new lab idea in the space below. Do that with three more changes.

Heat it	Freeze it	Reverse it	Double it
Bend it	Invert it	Poison it	Dehydrate it
Drown it	Stretch it	Fold it	Ignite it
Split it	Irradiate it	Oxidize it	Reduce it
Chill it	Speed it up	Color it	Grease it
Expand it	Substitute it	Remove it	Slow it down

        i. _____

_____

_____

_____

ii. _____

_____

_____

_____

iii. _____

_____

_____

_____

iv. _____

_____

_____

_____

Step Four • Create an Original Idea—Your Hypothesis

Your hypothesis should be stated as a prediction. You've done the basic experiment, you've made observations. Put two and two together and make an educated guess. **Be sure that your hypothesis can be measured and evaluated using an experiment.**

A. State your hypothesis in the space below. List the variable.

i. _____

_____

_____

_____

(Ask yourself, "Is this a prediction that can be measured?")

ii. Variable tested: _____

Quick Check • Evaluating Hypotheses

Listed below are four different proposed hypotheses. Read each one and decide if it is a hypothesis or not, and tell why you think so. Answers are found on the next page.

1. Smoker's Poll Among Teenagers

☐ Hypothesis   ☐ Try Again

Why: _____

_____

_____

2. I predict that the length of a metal rod directly affects the pitch it produces when it is vibrated.

☐ Hypothesis   ☐ Try Again

Why: _____

_____

_____

3. The Mighty Grand Canyon

☐ Hypothesis   ☐ Try Again

Why: _____

_____

_____

4. I predict that the humidity in a closed room, measured as percent water vapor, has no effect on the effectiveness of a Van de Graaff generator's ability to produce static electric sparks.

☐ Hypothesis   ☐ Try Again

Why: _____

_____

Quick Check • Evaluating Hypotheses

Listed below are four different proposed hypothses. Read each one and decide if it is a a true hypothesis or not and tell why you think so. *Some possible answers are listed below.*

1. Smoker's Poll Among Teenagers

[ ] Hypothesis   [✓] Try Again

Why: _A lot of teachers get sucked into thinking this is a good science fair project. It could be very good but in general the kids do not isolate a single variable or make a prediction._

2. I predict that the length of a metal rod directly affects the pitch it produces when it is vibrated.

[✓] Hypothesis   [ ] Try Again

Why: _The student makes a statement and provides a concrete way to measure and evaluate that statement._

3. The Mighty Grand Canyon

[ ] Hypothesis   [✓] Try Again

Why: _I am sure there are all kinds of studies about the Grand Canyon and its inhabitants currently under way, but unless the student is going to participate in the program, this is a report._

4. I predict that the humidity in a closed room, measured as percent water vapor, has no effect on the effectiveness of a Van de Graaff generator's ability to produce static electric sparks.

[✓] Hypothesis   [ ] Try Again

Why: Great. _A prediction is made and a way to measure that prediction is laid out in very clear terms. This kid is well on her way to a successful science fair project._

Scientific Method
· Step 2 ·
Gather Information

It's Due When ?!? • *B. K. Hixson*

"Children enter school as question marks and leave as periods."

• *Neil Postman*
Educator

Objectives of This Section

Doing research will help you settle into your project and get a better feel for the general topic. You have two main objectives for this section.

_____ 1. Identify the resources on the topic that are available to you, including:

    _____ A.   Contemporary Print Resources
    _____ B.   Other Print Resources
    _____ C.   Celluloid Resources
    _____ D.   Electronic Resources
    _____ E.   Human Resources

_____ 2. Use those resources to determine the following:

    _____ A.   Major Scientific Concepts
    _____ B.   Scientific Vocabulary
    _____ C.   The Historical Perspective, Scientists

Study Before You Start

A very successful and very wealthy businessman was nearing the end of his life on Earth and wanted desperately to take some of his considerable wealth with him.

He knelt down and began praying to the Lord who, surprising the man greatly, appeared beside him. The Lord said, "You have done very well with the gifts that I have given you; you have looked out for the those who were less fortunate than yourself. What can I do for you, my son?"

The man replied, "I know that I am near the end of my days here on Earth. You know that I began life as a very poor child and worked diligently to earn great wealth. The thought of going to Heaven and not having a thing to take with me is almost more than I can bear. Please, I know that everyone says that you can't take it with you but could you make an exception in my case?"

The Lord looked deep into the man's eyes and replied, "I will make an exception just this once. You can have just one suitcase." He touched the man gently on the head and then vanished.

Overjoyed, the man set about to purchase the largest suitcase that he could find and filled it with gold bars. Almost as soon as he was done packing an angel appeared and said, "It is time to go," and escorted the man to the Pearly Gates where he and his suitcase got into a long line.

When he finally got to the front of the line, Saint Peter looked down and said, "I am sorry sir, but we don't allow you to bring anything with you." The man assured him that the Lord himself had given him permission, so Peter agreed as long as the man would allow him to see what was in the suitcase.

With a large smile the man unzipped the bag and showed Peter the bars of gold. Upon seeing the contents, Peter started laughing uncontrollably. He summoned Gabriel, Moses, and several others who were nearby and they too started laughing.

Finally, the man couldn't stand it any longer and demanded to know what was so funny. With tears in his eyes, Peter took a deep breath and said, "You could have brought anything you wanted and you packed pavement!"

If only he had done his homework.

Locate Resources

There are several sources of information available to help you fill in the details from the previous page.

1. Print Resources

A. Contemporary
   (Magazines, Newspapers, Journals)

   i. _____

   ii. _____

   iii. _____

   iv. _____

   v. _____

   vi. _____

B. Reference
   (Books, Encyclopedias, Dictionaries, Textbooks)

   i. _____

   ii. _____

   iii. _____

   iv. _____

   v. _____

   vi. _____

2. Electronic Resources

A. Celluloid Resources
   (Films, Filmstrips, Videos)

   i. _____

   ii. _____

   iii. _____

   iv. _____

   v. _____

   vi. _____

YEP, LOOKS GOOD TO ME.

B. *Electronic Resources:*
   (Internet Web Site Addresses, DVD's, MP3's)

   i. _____

   ii. _____

   iii. _____

   iv. _____

   v. _____

   vi. _____

   vii. _____

   viii. _____

   ix. _____

   x. _____

3. Human Resources
   (Scientists, Engineers, Professionals, Professors, Teachers)

   i. _____

   ii. _____

   iii. _____

   iv. _____

   v. _____

   vi. _____

You may want to keep a record of all of your research and add it to the back of the report as an Appendix. Some teachers who are into volume think this is really cool. Others, like myself, find it a pain in the tuchus. No matter what you do, be sure to keep an accurate record of where you find data. If you quote from a report word for word, be sure to give proper credit with either a footnote or parenthetical reference. Failure to do so is deemed plagiarism, an ugly disease that attacks unimaginative folks.

Resource Synopsis Templates

A template is a standard pattern that you review and adapt for your own use. We have provided you with three different Resource Synopsis Templates so that as you pursue the research part of your Science Fair Project you will gather the information that will be most valuable to you.

As you read about your topic, watch videos, or interview scientists and other professionals, you will want to collect as much information about each source as possible. If you copy a passage or quote a person exactly, be sure to use quotation marks. If you rewrite the information into your own words, you will not need to use them. Make as many copies of the templates as you need. Keep all of your sources separate.

A. The first of these is the **Print Resource Synopsis Sheet.** Use it with resources that you *read* from printed materials. These are contemporary articles that would appear in magazines or popular books as well as definitions from dictionaries and passages taken from encyclopedias.

Quite often journals are given volume numbers. Newspapers not only have a date but also an issue number. All printed books will probably have an ISBN (International Serial Book Number) located on the first couple of pages for reference. You will need to copy the relevant information.

B. The second of these is the **Electronic Resource Synopsis Sheet.** It is to be used with resources that you *read or listen to* from media like CD's, Videos, DVD's, and so on. If you use the Internet to do your background research you will probably find online dictionaries, encyclopedias, reference sheets, biographies, and lots more. Record each Web site, key words, and the data. Do the same with more concrete resources that are stored on a single disk or videocassette.

C. The third of these is the **Human Resource Synopsis Sheet.** It is to be used with resources that you *talk* with, such as professionals and lay folks in the field. In addition to pumping them for information and ideas, find out how long they have been studying your topic, where they went to school, and if they have received any awards.

Print Resource Synopsis Sheet

A. Type of Media (circle one)

    Magazine   *Newspaper*   *Journal*   *Encyclopedia*

    Text Book   *Dictionary*   *Book*

B. Name/Title: _____

C. Title of Article/Chapter: _____

D. Publisher/Author: _____

E. ISBN (Books Only): _____

F. Year Published: _____ Month: _____

G. Volume #: _____ Pages Referenced: _____

H. Synopsis of Ideas: _____

_____

_____

_____

_____

_____

_____

_____

I. Print Resource Synopsis, page ____ of ____.

Electronic Resource Synopsis Sheet

A. Type of Media (circle one)
    Internet   *CD/Video*   *DVD*   *MP3*

B. Web site/Title: _____

C. Title of *CD/Video*, etc.: _____

D. Publisher/Author: _____

E. Internet Address: _____

F. Year Produced: _____ Volume #: _____

G. Synopsis of Ideas: _____

_____

_____

_____

_____

_____

_____

_____

_____

H. Electronic Resource Synopsis, page _____ of _____.

Human Resource Synopsis Sheet

A. Type of Professional (circle one)

    Scientist   *Engineer*   *Professor*   *Doctor*
    Teacher   *Librarian*   *Other*

B. Name: _____

C. Title/Position : _____

D. Employer: _____

E. Date Interviewed: _____/_____/_____

F. Years in Field: _____ Degree(s): _____

G. Awards: _____

H. Synopsis of Ideas: _____

_____

_____

_____

_____

_____

_____

_____

_____

I. Human Resource Synopsis, page _____ of _____.

Gathering Information

Read about your topic and find out what we already know. Check books, videos, the Internet, and movies, talk with experts in the field, and molest an encyclopedia or two. Gather as much information as you can before you begin planning your experiment.

In particular, there are several things you will want to pay special attention to and that should accompany any good science fair project.

A. Major Scientific Concepts
Be sure you research and explain the main idea(s) that is/are driving your experiment. It may be a law of physics or a chemical rule or an explanation of an aspect of plant physiology. When did we first learn about this idea, and who is responsible for getting us this far? You need to give a historical perspective with names, dates, countries, awards, and other recognition.

B. Scientific Words
As you use scientific terms in your paper, you should also define them in the margins of the paper or in a glossary at the end of the report. You cannot assume that everyone knows about geothermal energy transmutation in sulfur-loving bacterium. Be prepared to define some new terms for them. Whenever possible, look each word up twice, in two different resources and compare the definitions. You'll occasionally be surprised by what you read.

Again, we have provided you with two different templates so that as you develop the research part of your science fair project you will gather the information that will be most valuable to you. These sheets are designed to help you organize your thoughts and give you some ideas of what to look for on your topic. When you prepare your lab report, you may want to include the background information outlined on the next three pages.

Building a Research Foundation

A. *Major Scientific Concepts (Two is plenty.)*

    i. _____

_____

_____

    ii. _____

_____

_____

B. *Scientific Words (No more than 10)*

    i. _____

    ii. _____

    iii. _____

    iv. _____

    v. _____

    vi. _____

    vii. _____

    viii. _____

    ix. _____

    x. _____

Scientific Concept Template

A. Major Scientific Concept: _____

_____

_____

B. Discovered by: _____

(Scientist's Name)

C. Country: _____ Year: _____

D. Opposition to Idea: _____

_____

_____

E. Awards: _____

F. Miscellaneous Info: _____

_____

_____

Vocabulary Word Template

A. Scientific Word: _____

B. Pronunciation: _____

C. Origin: _____
    (Greek, Latin, French, Contemporary)

D. Meaning: _____
    (The original meaning or root of the word)

_____

E. Definition 1: _____

_____

Source for Definition 1
Name: _____ Page: _____

F. Definition 2: _____

_____

Source for Definition 2
Name: _____ Page: _____

Scientific Method
• Step 3 •
Design Your Experiment

"Creative thinking may simply mean the realization that there is no particular virtue in doing things the way they have always been done."

• Rudolph Flesch
Educator

Objectives of This Section

A well-designed experiment will allow you to collect accurate data the first time you experiment. You will also be able to replicate your experiment and retrieve supporting data the second and third time you experiment.

_____ 1. Outline each step of the experiment. Make sure you are testing a single variable.

_____ 2. Evaluate the lab activity for potential safety problems and make preparations, if necessary.

_____ 3. Prepare your data tables.

_____ 4. Acquire all of the lab materials you need to perform the experiment at least three times.

_____ 5. Present a complete experimental design to the adult who is helping you with this process, including a master materials list, experimental procedure, and completed data table templates.

Special Alert

In the mid 60s, F.B.I. Director Hoover was reviewing a typed letter that he had just dictated to his secretary. He didn't like the format she had used, thinking it was messy, so he scribbled, "Watch the borders" on the bottom of it and asked her to retype it and send it out immediately.

She did exactly as she was instructed and sent the letter out to all of the top agents in the field. For the next two weeks agents were put on special alert along the Mexican and Canadian borders.

When you outline your experiment do your best to avoid ambiguity.

Experimental Procedure Outline

This sheet is designed to help you outline the steps of your experiment. If you need more space, make a copy of this page to finish your outline. When you are done with this sheet, review it with an adult, and make any necessary changes.

In the spaces below, list each of the steps you are going to take to complete your experiment. This is an outline so you can abbreviate. You will use this work sheet as the foundation to fill out and complete your final experimental procedure.

1. _____

_____

2. _____

_____

3. _____

_____

4. _____

_____

5. _____

_____

6. _____

_____

7. _____

_____

8. _____

_____

9. _____

_____

10. _____

_____

Evaluate Safety Concerns

There are some very specific safety questions you need to ask, and prepare for, depending on the needs of your experiment. If you find that you need to prepare for any of these safety concerns, place a check mark next to the letter. These concerns and safety checks need to be written into your final procedure.

___ A. Goggles & Eyewash Station

If you are mixing chemicals or working with materials that might splinter or produce flying objects, goggles and an eyewash station or sink with running water should be available.

___ B. Ventilation

If you are mixing chemicals that could produce fire, smoke, fumes, or obnoxious odors, you need to use a vented hood or go outside and perform the experiment in the fresh air.

___ C. Fire Blanket or Fire Extinguisher

If you are working with potentially combustible chemicals or electricity, a fire blanket and extinguisher nearby are a must.

___ D. Chemical Disposal

If your experiment produces a poisonous chemical or there are chemical-filled tissues (as in dissected animals), you may need to make arrangements to dispose of the by-products from your lab.

___ E. Electricity

If you are working with materials and developing an idea that uses electricity, make sure that the wires are in good repair, that the electrical demand does not exceed the capacity of the supply, and that your work area is grounded.

___ F. Emergency Phone Numbers

Look up and record the following phone numbers. Fire Department: _____ , Poison Control: _____ , and Hospital: _____. Post them in an easy-to-find location.

It's Due When ?!? • B. K. Hixson

Prepare Data Tables

Finally, you will want to prepare your data tables and have them ready to go before you start your experiment. Each data table should be easy to understand and easy for you to use.

A good data table has a **title** that describes the information being collected, and it identifies the **variable** and the **unit** being collected on each data line. The variable is *what* you are measuring and the unit is *how* you are measuring it. They are usually written like this:

Variable (unit), or to give you some examples:

Time (seconds)
Distance (meters)
Electricity (volts)

An example of a well-prepared data table looks like the sample below. We've cut the data table into thirds because the book is too small to display the whole line.

Determining the Boiling Point of Compound X_1

Time (min.)	0	1	2	3	4	5	6
Temp. (°C)							

Time (min.)	7	8	9	10	11	12	13
Temp. (°C)							

Time (min.)	14	15	16	17	18	19	20
Temp. (°C)							

Data Table Templates • Single Test

Title: _____

Variable / V: _____ Unit (U): _____

Constant / C _____ Unit (U): _____

Title:

V(U)							
C(U)							

This data table would be used when you are testing a single thing, like the rate that a solution boils, or the distance an object travels over time.

Data Table Templates • Multiple Tests

Title: _____

Variable /V: _____ Unit(U): _____

Constant /C_____ Unit (U): _____

Title:

C(U)	V(U)$_1$	V(U)$_2$	V(U)$_3$

This data table would be used when you are testing multiple things, like the response of four different plants to light, or the distance several objects travel over time.

Master Lab Materials List

List the *all* of the materials you need to complete your experiment in the table below. Be sure to list multiples if you will need more than one item. For example: 10 straws.

Many science materials double as household items in their spare time. For each of the materials you have listed below, see if it is possible to find that material around your house. If it is, mark the circle with a check. For things that you can't find around your house or apartment, but you could purchase at a grocery, hardware, or speciality store, put a check in those circles, also.

Qty.	Material	Home	Grocery	Hardware	Other
		O	O	O	O
		O	O	O	O
		O	O	O	O
		O	O	O	O
		O	O	O	O
		O	O	O	O
		O	O	O	O
		O	O	O	O
		O	O	O	O
		O	O	O	O
		O	O	O	O
		O	O	O	O
		O	O	O	O
		O	O	O	O
		O	O	O	O

It's Due When ?!? • *B. K. Hixson*

Difficult-to-Find Lab Materials

Once you have ruled out the house, school, grocery, hardware, and general merchandise store, you are most likely going to have to purchase the remainder of your supplies from a science supply company.

There are lots of good companies out there and there are a lot of ethical folks in the business. Several of them are my friends and I do business with them as well. However, it goes without saying that there are also a few sharks lurking in the waters. If you have the time, go online, order catalogs, and compare prices and quality.

When you are ready to order, use the order form in the catalog, or do one of your own. Inspect the order when it arrives and don't be afraid to squeak if everything is not just right.

Material	Qty.	Source	$
1.			
2.			
3.			
4.			
5.			
6.			
7.			
8.			
9.			
10.			
11.			
12.			

Recommended Materials Suppliers

For the more difficult items on your list, we have selected, for your convenience, a small but respectable list of suppliers who will meet your needs in a timely and economical manner. Call for a catalog or quote on the item you are looking for and they will be happy to give you a hand.

Loose in the Lab
9462 South 560 West
Sandy, UT 84070
Phone 1-888-403-1189
Fax 1-801-568-9586
www.looseinthelab.com
General Science

Delta Education
80 NW Boulevard
Nashua, NH 03601
Phone 1-800-442-5444
Fax 1-800-282-9560
www.delta-ed.com
General Science

NASCO
901 Jonesville Ave.
Fort Atkinson, WI 53538
Phone 1-414-563-2446
Fax 1-920-563-8296
www.nascofa.com
General Science

Ward's Scientific
5100 W Henrietta Road
Rochester, NY 14692
Phone 800-387-7822
Fax 1-716-334-6174
www.wardsci.com
General Science

Educational Innovations
362 Main
Norwalk, CT 06851
Phone 1-888-912-7474
Fax 1-203-629-2739
www.teachersource.com
General Science

Frey Scientific
100 Paragon Parkway
Mansfield, OH 44903
Phone 1-800-225-FREY
Fax 1-419-589-1546
www.freyscientific.com
General Science

More Recommended Materials Suppliers

Edmund Scientific
101 E. Gloucester Pike
Barrington, NJ 08007
Phone 1-(800) 728-6999
Fax 1-856-547-3292
www.edmundscientific.com
General Science

Sargent Welch Scientific Co.
911 Commerce Court
Buffalo Grove, IL 60089
Phone 800-727-4368
Fax 1-800-676-2540
www.sargentwelch.com
General Science

William Mark Corp
112 N Harvard #229
Claremont, CA. 91711
Phone 909-621-6823
Fax 909-621-4247
www. x-zylo.com
Flying Widgets

Ohaus Corporation
1980 Chapin Rd.
Pine Brook, NJ 07058
Phone 800-672-7722
Fax 1- 800-672-7722
www.ohaus.com
Instruments

AIMS Education Foundation
PO Box 8210
Fresno, CA.   93747
Phone 888-SEE-AIMS
Fax 1-559-255-6396
www. AIMSedu.org
General Science

Pitsco
Box 1708
Pittsburg, KS. 66762
Phone 800-835-0686
Fax 1-800-533-8104
www.pitsco.com
General Science

ETA Cuisenaire Co
500 Greenview Ct.
Vernon Hills, IL 60061
Phone 800-445-5985
Fax 1-800-382-9326
www.etacuisinaire.com
General Science

DK Publishing
95 Madison Avenue
NY, NY 10016
Phone 1 877-342-5357

www.dk.com
Publisher

And One Last Page

Nebraska Scientific
3823 Leanvenworth St.
Omaha, NE 68105
Phone 800-228-7117
Fax 1-402-346-2216
www. nebraskascientific.com
Science Fair Materials

Estes Industries
1295 H St.
Penrose, Co. 81240
Phone 800-525-7561
Fax 1-719-372-3217
www.estesrockets.com
Rockets

Fisher Scientific
485 S. Frontage Rd.
Burr Ridge, Il 60521
Phone 800-955-1177
Fax 1-800-955-0740
www.fisheredu.com
General Science

Flinn Scientific
PO Box 219
Batavia, Il. 60510
Phone 1-800 452-1261
Fax 1-630-879-6962
www.flinnsci.com
Chemistry

Hubbard Scientific
401 Hickory St.
Fort Collins, Co. 80524
Phone 800-446-8767
Fax 1-970-484-1198
www.hubbardscott.com
General Science

Insect Lore
PO Box 1535
Shafter, Ca. 93263
Phone 800-LIVE BUG
Fax 1-661-746-0334
www.insectlore.com
Publisher

Boreal Labs
777 E. Park Dr.
Tonawanda, NY 14150
Phone 800-828-7777
Fax 1-800-828-3299
www. sciencekit.com
General Science

TOPS Learning Systems
10070 S. Mulino Rd.
Canby,Or. 97013
Phone 888-773-9755
Fax 1-503-266-5200
www.topscience.org
General Science

It's Due When ?!? • B. K. Hixson

Proposed Experiment Design

This sheet is the guide you will use when you are conducting your experiment. It is your road map; prepare it well. You will need to do the following:

A. List all of the materials you are going to need and use. Include the quantities, even if you only need one of each item.

B. List each step of the experiment in the order you are going to do it. Be sure to incorporate safety concerns where they are appropriate. Be thorough in your directions; do not allow for guesswork on the part of anyone who is replicating your work.

C. Prepare your data tables on separate sheets of paper. Refer to them in the step-by-step procedure by stating "Record data in accompanying data table titled: _____."

Lab Materials

Quantity   Items

_____   _____

_____   _____

_____   _____

_____   _____

Procedure

1. _____

_____

_____

2. _____

_____

_____

Scientific Method
• Step 4 •
Conduct the Experiment

"I find the great thing in this world is not so much where we stand, as in what direction we are moving: To reach the post of heaven, we must sail sometimes with the wind and sometimes against it— but we must sail, and not drift, nor lie at anchor."

• Oliver Wendell Holmes

Objectives of This Section

Show time!

____ 1. Do the lab and follow the procedure. Record any changes that you make during the lab.

____ 2. Observe all safety rules.

____ 3. Collect and record data immediately.

____ 4. Repeat the experiment several times.

____ 5. Prepare for extended experiments.

The Chicken Cannon

When the British were designing their high-speed train, they became concerned about the consequence of accidentally hitting a bird at 180 m.p.h. as the train zipped down the track.

After quite a bit of discussion and some research, they discovered that the American space program, NASA, had designed a cannon that fired chickens at the windshield of the Space Shuttle to test its effectiveness for the very same occurrence.

The British borrowed the cannon and were quite excited to try it out on the newly designed, state-of-the-art windshields they intended to use on the new, high-speed trains. They loaded the gun and fired the first chicken at the windshield, only to watch in complete horror as the chicken not only shattered the windshield, but also destroyed the conductor's chair and imbedded itself in the back wall of the cabin.

Needless to say they immediately sent all the data back to NASA and asked them for any advice that the scientists in the United States might have to help them with their dilemma. The Americans evaluated that data and quickly replied with three words:

"Thaw the chicken."

As you begin to experiment, double check your procedure and make any necessary adjustments.

Safety Overview

It's time to get going. You've generated a hypothesis, collected the materials, written out the procedure, checked the safety issues, and prepared your data tables. Fire it up. Here's the short list of things to remember as you experiment.

____ A. Follow the Procedure, Record Any Changes

Follow your own directions specifically as you wrote them. If you find the need to change the procedure once you are into the experiment, that's fine; it's part of the process. Make sure to keep detailed records of the changes. When you repeat the experiment a second or third time, follow the new directions exactly.

____ B. Observe Safety Rules

It's easier to complete the lab activity if you are in the lab rather than the emergency room.

____ C. Record Data Immediately

Collect temperatures, distances, voltages, revolutions, and any other variables and immediately record them into your data table. Do not think you will be able to remember them and fill everything in after the lab is completed.

____ D. Repeat the Experiment Several Times

The more data that you collect, the better. It will give you a larger data base and your averages are more meaningful. As you do multiple experiments, be sure to identify each data set by date and time so you can separate them out.

____ E. Prepare for Extended Experiments

Some experiments require days or weeks to complete, particularly those with plants and animals or the growing of crystals. Prepare a safe place for your materials so your experiment can continue undisturbed while you collect the data. Be sure you've allowed enough time for your due date.

Lab Safety

Since you are on your own in this journey we thought it prudent to share some basic wisdom and experience in the safety department. Contained herein are ten guidelines that you should follow as you do any experiment. Read them over and incorporate the ideas into your project.

Read the Instructions

An interesting concept, especially if you are a teenager. Take a minute before you jump in and get going to read all of the instructions as well as warnings. If you do not understand something, stop and ask an adult for help.

Clean Up All Messes

Keep your lab area clean. It will make it easier to put everything away at the end and may also prevent contamination and the subsequent germination of a species of mutant tomato bug larva. You will also find that chemicals perform with more predictability if they are not poisoned with foreign molecules.

Organize

Translation: Put it back where you got it. If you need any more clarification, there is an opening at the landfill for you.

Lab Safety

Dispose of Poisons Properly

This will not be much of a problem with labs that use, study, split, and mix light. However, if you happen to wander over into one of the many disciplines that incorporates the use of chemicals, then we suggest that you use great caution with the materials and definitely dispose of any and all poisons properly.

Practice Good Fire Safety

If there is a fire in the room, notify an adult immediately. If an adult is not in the room and the fire is manageable, smother the outbreak with a fire blanket or use a fire extinguisher. When the fire is contained, immediately send someone to find an adult. If, for any reason, you happen to catch on fire, **REMEMBER: Stop, Drop, and Roll.** Never run; it adds oxygen to the fire, making it burn faster, and it also scares the bat guano out of the neighbors when they see the neighbor kids running down the block doing an imitation of a campfire marshmallow without the stick.

Protect Your Skin

It is a good idea to always wear protective gloves whenever you are working with chemicals. If you do happen to spill a chemical on your skin, notify an adult immediately and then flush the area with water for 15 minutes. It's unlikely, but if irritation develops, have your parents or another responsible adult look at it. If it appears to be of concern, contact a physician. Take any information that you have about the chemical with you.

It's Due When ?!? • B. K. Hixson

Lab Safety

Save Your Nosehairs

Sounds like a cause celeb, L.A. style, but it is really good advice. To smell a chemical to identify it, hold the open container six to ten inches down and away from your nose. Make a clockwise circular motion with your hand over the opening of the container, "wafting" some of the fumes toward your nose. This will allow you to safely smell some of the fumes without exposing yourself to a large dose of anything noxious. This technique may help prevent a nose bleed or your lungs from accidentally getting burned by chemicals.

Wear Goggles if Appropriate

If the lab asks you to heat or mix chemicals, be sure to wear protective eye wear. Also have an eye wash station or running water available. You never know when something is going to splatter, splash, or react unexpectedly and it is better to look like a nerd and be prepared than schedule a trip down to pick out a Seeing Eye™ dog. If you do happen to accidentally get chemicals in your eye, flush the area for 15 minutes. If any irritation or pain develops, immediately go see a doctor.

THIS TASTES REALLY FUNNY.

Lose the Comedy Routine

You should have plenty of time scheduled during your day to mess around, but science lab is not one of them. Horseplay breaks glassware, spills chemicals, and creates unnecessary messes—things that parents do not appreciate; trust us on this one.

No Eating

Do not eat while performing a lab. Putting your food in the lab area contaminates your food and the experiment. This makes for bad science and worse indigestion. Avoid poisoning yourself and goobering up your lab ware by observing this rule.

Happy and safe experimenting!

Scientific Method
• Step 5 •
Gathering & Evaluating the Data

"Man, unlike any other thing, organic or inorganic in the universe, grows beyond his work, walks up the stairs of his concepts, emerges ahead of his accomplishments."

• John Steinbeck
   Author

Objectives of This Section

This is where you bring the bacon home. Taking the data that you collect and connecting it to a logical conclusion is at the very heart of the scientific method.

_____ 1. Fill in the data tables you have prepared.

_____ 2. Use the data to create graphs that will quickly display the information you have collected.

_____ 3. Collect and prepare other forms of data—recordings, photos, drawings, and so on—that will support your hypothesis.

_____ 4. Develop descriptions, explanations, predictions, and models using evidence.

_____ 5. Think critically and logically to make the relationships between evidence and explanations.

_____ 6. Recognize and analyze alternative explanations and predictions.

Free Tickets

Three engineers and three accountants are traveling by train to a conference. At the station, the three accountants each buy tickets and watch as the three engineers buy only a single ticket. "How are three people going to travel on only one ticket?" asks an accountant.

"Watch and you'll see," answers an engineer.

They all board the train. The accountants take their respective seats, but all three engineers cram into a restroom and close the door behind them. Shortly after the train has departed, the conductor comes around collecting tickets.

He knocks on the restroom door and says, "Ticket, please." The door opens just a crack and a single arm emerges with ticket in hand. The conductor takes it and moves on.

The accountants saw this and agreed it was quite a clever idea. So after the conference, the accountants decide to copy the engineers on the return trip and save some money.

When they get to the station, they buy a single ticket for the return trip. To their astonishment, the engineers buy no tickets at all.

" How are you guys going to travel without a ticket?" says one perplexed accountant.

"Watch and you'll see," answers an engineer.

When they board the train, the three accountants cram into a restroom and the three engineers cram into one nearby. The train departs. Shortly afterward, one of the engineers leaves his restroom and walks over to the restroom where the accountants are hiding. He knocks on the door and says, "Ticket please."

When you are doing your lab work, be sure you collect enough data to draw an accurate conclusion.

Types of Graphs

This section will give you some ideas on how you can use graphs to display the information you are going to collect as a graph. A graph is simply a picture of the data that you gathered portrayed in a manner that is quick and easy to reference. There are four kinds of graphs described on the next two pages. If you find you need a leg up in the graphing department, Loose in the Lab has a book about *Data Tables & Graphing*. It will guide you through the process.

Line and Bar Graphs

These are the most common kinds of graphs. The most consistent variable is plotted on the "x", or horizontal, axis and the more temperamental variable is plotted along the "y", or vertical, axis. Each data point on a line graph is recorded as a dot and then all of the dots are connected to form a picture of the data. A bar graph starts on the horizontal axis and moves up to the data line.

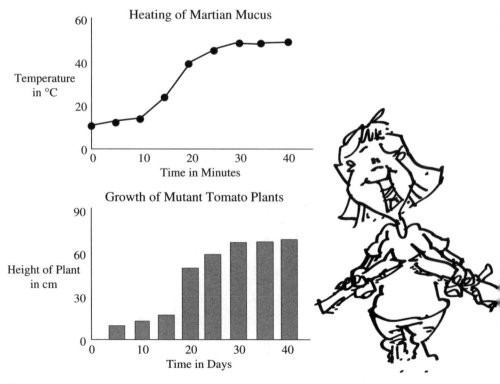

Types of Graphs

Best Fit Graphs

A best fit graph was created to show averages or trends rather than specific data points. The data that has been collected is plotted just as on a line graph, but instead of drawing a line from point to point to point, which sometimes is impossible anyway, you just free hand a line that hits "most of the data."

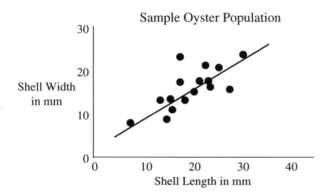

Pie Graphs

Pie graphs are used to show relationships between different groups. All of the data is totaled up and a percentage is determined for each group. The pie is then divided to show the relationship of one group to another.

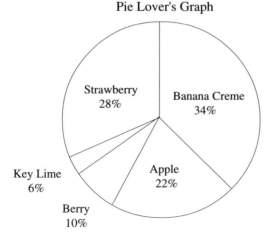

Other Kinds of Data

1. Written Notes & Observations

This is the age-old technique used by all scientists. Record your observations in a lab book. Written notes can be made quickly as the experiment is proceeding, and they can then be expounded upon later.

2. Drawings

Quick sketches as well as fully developed drawings can be used as a way to report data for a science experiment. Be sure to title each drawing and, if possible, label what it is that you are looking at.

3. Photographs, Videotapes, and Audiotapes

Usually better than drawings, quicker, and more accurate, but you do have the added expense and time of developing the film. However, they can often capture images and details that are not usually seen by the naked eye.

THAT'S IT... NICE RHINOCEROS ... OK, NO DON'T CHARGE.

4. The Experiment Itself

Some of the best data you can collect and present is the actual experiment itself. Nothing will speak more effectively for you than the plants you grew, the specimens you collected, or that big pile of tissue that was an armadillo you peeled from the tread of an 18-wheeler.

Evaluating Your Data

Once your data is collected, it is time to sit down and let it tell a story. Let it describe the phenomena that you just witnessed. The following pages have some guide sheets that should help you evaluate your data and create interpretations from the numbers and squiggles that you collected.

The first sheet is going to ask you to describe, evaluate, predict, and create models from your data. We will state the question that will be posed and give you an example to help clarify the direction you should be going.

1. Descriptions
What does the data that you collected allow you to describe about your experiment?

This is almost a pure kind of observation. Think of yourself as a *reporter* in this instance. You are not trying to figure out why something happened or what it means in the context of world religion, you are just looking and reporting what you see. "Wow, that's big, it's very flat, smells like spinach souffle, and the sound is similar to the howling of a coyote." Stuff like that. Here are some more examples.

A. If you are looking at a graph of the temperature of a solution produced when two chemicals are mixed together, a description could be: "The heat released by the reaction of the two chemicals warmed the solution to 15 degrees Celsius in 5 minutes." Or . . .

B. If you are doing a chromatography experiment: "The colors produced by the super-fed marigold leaves were dark green, green, light green, dark yellow, and a thin band of orange."

C. And finally, from our new airplane-design competition: "The second wing provided additional lift that could be easily seen as the plane ascended toward the ceiling at twice the rate of any of the other previous plane designs."

Evaluating Data • Some Examples

2. Explanations

How does the data that you collected allow you to explain what you observed about your experiment?

You are now playing the thinking person's game. Think of yourself as an *analyst* in this instance. This requires that you evaluate the data and describe why it did what it did. An example:

A. "The plane rose toward the ceiling faster <u>because</u> the curve across the top of the airfoil had been increased by 7 degrees." You tell why it did what it did. Or. . .

B. "The super-fed marigolds had access to extra selenium in the soil that <u>is believed to be</u> a principal component in Chlorophyll C. Chlorophyll C produces a dark yellow band in chromatography experiments."

C. "The temperature of the water in the solution increases because the energy that the molecule was using to hold the atoms together was released as heat and that heat was absorbed by the water."

3. Predictions

What predictions, if any, are you able to make by using the data that you collected in your experiment?

Grab your crystal ball and make a prediction. Think of yourself as a *weatherman* in this instance. You are taking the existing data and using it to decide what might happen if . . .

A. "Given the heat of reaction in the original experiment it is entirely probable that doubling the amount of chemical could very easily double the temperature produced."

B. You haven't done the experiment, but based on what you have seen so far you are guessing or predicting what will happen next.

4. Models

Are there any models that you can create that would describe or explain the data and findings of your experiment?

A model can be a physical example, like a model of a molecule constructed from styrofoam balls and toothpicks or a set of data that represents a general trend like a model of a hurricane. It is not the exact hurricane but a representative model based on a lot of data. Some other examples:

A. "By taking chromatography samples from over 200 super-fed marigolds, we have developed a generalized model of what the color-band sequence would probably look like."

B. "Having measured the temperature increase of 1 liter of water, we have developed a mathematical model that allows us to predict the end temperature of the solution when any amount of chemical is mixed."

C. "Combining the two plane designs, we created a physical model that meets the rate-of-climb demands without stalling, that we were hoping to achieve."

Hopefully, that was more helpful than confusing. The work sheet we would like you to fill out is on the next page.

Evaluating Data Work Sheet

1. Descriptions

What does the data that you collected allow you to describe about your experiment?

_____

_____

_____

_____

2. Explanations

How does the data that you collected allow you to explain what you observed about your experiment?

_____

_____

_____

_____

3. Predictions

What predictions, if any, are you able to make by using the data that you collected in your experiment?

_____

_____

_____

_____

4. Models

Are there any models that you can create that would describe or explain the data and findings of your experiment?

_____

_____

_____

Logically Connect Data with Explanations

Think critically and logically to make the relationships between evidence and explanations. One way to do this is to use the following sheet to help you sort out your thoughts.

1. Evidence

The evidence that I have supporting/refuting (choose one) my hypothesis is ... _____

_____

_____

_____

2. Explanations

The reasons that this evidence supports/refutes (choose one) my hypothesis are:

A._____

_____

_____

_____

B._____

_____

_____

_____

C._____

_____

_____

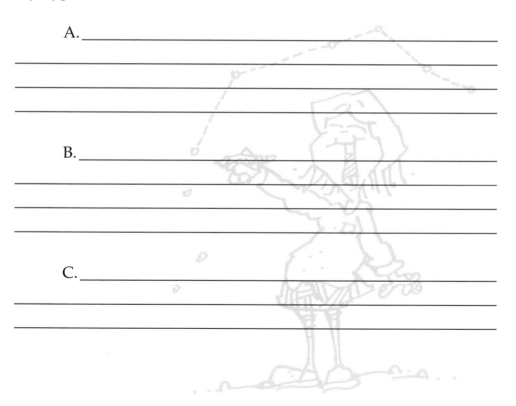

Explore Alternatives to Your Explanation

It is also very important for scientists to examine their work and be able to recognize and analyze alternative explanations and predictions that become evident from their research. This does not always happen but should be explored.

1. Evidence
The evidence that I have supporting/refuting (choose one) my hypothesis is ... _____

_____

_____

2. Alternative Explanations
In addition to the primary explanations I have given that this evidence supports/refutes (choose one) my hypothesis, there are other possible explanations that require more research and thought but may be just as viable.

A._____

_____

_____

B._____

_____

_____

C._____

_____

_____

3. Modified Experiment

To examine this alternative explanation I would modify the original experiment by ...

_____

_____

_____

_____

_____

_____

_____

_____

Scientific Method
• Step 6 •
Present Your Ideas

It's Due When ?!? • B. K. Hixson

"The pure magnitude of such a copious assertion is far too sagacious for my diminutive comprehension. It is merely corroborative detail intended to give artistic verisimilitude to an otherwise bald and unconvincing narrative."

• Geoff Nielson

Objectives of This Section

This is where all the hard work pays off. We are going to assume that you not only have to do an experiment but also prepare a report, a display, and present the project orally.

_____ 1. Prepare a thorough lab write-up. Start with the abstract and wind up with a glossary at the end with all the trimmings.

_____ 2. Create a visual presentation of your project. Use this display to accompany your oral presentation and also present it as part of the Science Fair.

_____ 3. Outline an oral presentation of your project and give it to your class in the allotted amount of time.

True Bravery

A young man sat down to take his college philosophy final. When he opened the cover of the exam, the question "What is courage?" stared back from the top of the page at him.

He thought for a moment and then wrote two words, "This is." He then turned his exam in, much to the amazement of his peers, after only using three minutes of the allotted two hours, and walked out the door of the lecture hall.

Not only should you dare to be creative in producing original ideas, but also you should strive to make original presentations of the data that is recovered. Hopefully, you have a teacher who would be willing to throw her entire grading system out the window if a student shows remarkable originality in the presentation of his or her ideas.

Then again, you may be sitting in the class of an old fuddy-duddy and anything original scares the pee waddlings out of him. Guess you have one last, little bit of research to do. What kind of teacher do you have?

By the way, the kid got an A.

Written Report Checklist

First up is the written report, also called your lab write-up. After you compile or sort the data you have collected during the experiment and evaluate the results, you will be able to come to a conclusion about your hypothesis. Remember, disproving an idea is as valuable as proving it.

This sheet is designed to help you write up your science fair project and present your data in an organized manner. This is a final checklist for you.

To prepare your write-up, your science fair report should include the following components:

_____ a.   binder
_____ b.   cover page, title, & your name
_____ c.   abstract (one paragraph summary)
_____ d.   table of contents with page numbers
_____ e.   hypothesis or question
_____ f.   background information
                     concepts
                     word definitions
                     history or scientists
_____ g.   list of materials used
_____ h.   experimental procedure
                     written description
                     photo or drawing of setup
_____ i.   data collected
                     data tables
                     graphs
                     photos or drawings
_____ j.   conclusions and findings
_____ k.   glossary of terms
_____ l.   references

The outlines on the following pages will make sure that you don't leave anything out in the final report.

The Abstract

The abstract is a one paragraph summary of your project. It is used by scientists doing research to quickly review a paper and decide if it has any information in it that will help them with their research. It is also used by librarians and other people who catalog and store information so that they can classify your work and place it with other similar kinds of papers.

Your abstract needs to meet the following criteria:

___ No longer than one paragraph
___ States your question
___ States your conclusion

Rough draft: _____

_____

_____

_____

_____

_____

_____

_____

Be sure to have at least two people proofread your final abstract. Copy or type your final version on a separate, clean sheet of white paper to be included in your report.

The Table of Contents

The Table of Contents is actually one of the last things you want to put together on your report. Gather all of the components up, arrange them, number the pages and then fill in the space to the right.

You may choose to personalize the categories that we listed below to make them more specific to your project. For example, instead of "concepts" you may want to list "principles of aerodynamics," if your report is on flight. Also, the titles from the data tables and graphs you created should be used.

Section Heading	Page #
cover page, title, & your name	____
abstract (one paragraph summary)	____
table of contents with page numbers	____
hypothesis or question	____
background information	
concepts	____
word definitions	____
history or scientists	____
list of materials used	____
experimental procedure	
written description	____
photo or drawing of setup	____
data collected	
data tables	____
graphs	____
photos or drawings	____
conclusions and findings	____
glossary of terms	____
references	____

Hypothesis

Now is not the time to change this piece of work. Put the title, Hypothesis, at the top of the page and then refer to page 35 in this book. Be sure to have at least two people proofread your final draft. When it is clean and ready to go, your final version should be presented on a separate, clean sheet of white paper to be included in your report.

Background Information

1. Concepts, History and/or Scientists

Refer to page 50 for review. On a separate sheet of paper, write the law(s) or concept(s) as it/they appear(s) in the book, encyclopedia, or journal that you are using. Enclose the concept in quotes and list your source of this information immediately afterward. Include title, author, and page number.

On a separate sheet of paper, you may want to include either some background information about the evolution of your idea or a very brief synopsis of a famous scientist who may have contributed significantly. For example, if you are doing a project on electric motors, then Michael Faraday would be a logical reference. If you are working with solar cells, no one scientist stands out, but there is a very clear history of how these have evolved over the years.

Write the scientist's name or topic in capital letters. Write one or two brief paragraphs. Include title, author, and page number of any books that you used for reference.

2. Word definitions

Refer to page 51 for review. On a separate sheet of paper, write the vocabulary words as they appear in the glossary, encyclopedia, or dictionary that you are using. The definition of the word should immediately follow the word. List your source of this information immediately afterward. Include title and page number of the reference you are using.

Materials

Refer to pages 60 and 61 in this book and be sure to have at least two people proofread your final draft. When it is ready to go, your final list of materials should be presented on a separate, clean sheet of white paper to be included in your report. Sound familiar?

Put the title, Materials, at the top of the page and then list all of the items that you used and the quantities in the order that you used them.

Quantity   Items

_____   _____

_____   _____

_____   _____

_____   _____

_____   _____

_____   _____

Experimental Procedure

You will, first of all, want to produce the original procedure that you proposed and used. Each step of the procedure should have its own number. If you followed the procedure exactly as you wrote it, great. However, a lot of kids find that once they get into the project they couldn't foresee all of the glitches, bumps in the road, and problems that would arise.

A good final procedure will show:

      a. where changes had to be made,
      b. why they had to be made,
      c. and how they influenced the evaluation of the hypothesis and it acceptance or rejection.

Data Collected

1. Data tables. These should be inserted in the final draft where they are appropriate to explain the conclusions. This can be a separate section after the Experimental Procedure or incorporated as part of the Conclusions. They need to have a title, variable with unit, constant with unit, the data, and be presented in a very neat and orderly manner. You should always print your data tables if you are doing them by hand or use a computer. Draw lines with a ruler, or again, use a computer.

2. Graphs should immediately follow the data tables. The title, variable with unit, constant with unit, and the data should be identical to the information in the data table. The graphs are also to be presented in a neat and orderly manner. You should always print your information if you are doing it by hand or use a computer. Draw lines with a ruler, or again, use a computer.

3. Photos and drawings must have labels (titles) and show scale so the reader can get a sense of proportion. Use a border to define your picture and draw in ink whenever possible.

4. Notes should be taken in neat, legible hand writing. If they are taken in the field and you are running from the volcano as it is exploding and showering you with molten debris, then retype or copy the notes when you get to a more relaxed setting. However, be sure to include the original set of notes.

5. Sound recordings, videotapes, and MP3's should be clearly labeled. If an audio tape is recorded, a typed transcript of the information that you collected should also be included in your data section.

Conclusions & Findings

Begin by making a definitive statement about your hypothesis. I was/was not able to support my hypothesis. Then you are going to want to explain, using the guide sheets that were provided on pages 85 and 86 to assist you.

It's Due When ?!? • *B. K. Hixson*

1. Show the relationship between the data you collected and your hypothesis.

2. Use descriptions, models, explanations, and other pieces of supportive evidence to support and/or refute your hypothesis.

3. Take a good, hard look at your data, then recognize and analyze alternative explanations that may be possible due to the data you collected.

Be sure to have at least two people proofread your final conclusion. Copy or type your final version on a separate, clean sheet of white paper to be included in your report.

Glossary of Terms

On a separate sheet of paper, write the vocabulary words and other terms you used in your report. As with your background section, the definition should immediately follow the word. List your source of this information immediately afterward. Include title and page number of the reference you are using.

References

This is a good time to include the reference sheets that you collected during Step 2 of the process. List all of the significant resources that you used in the preparation of your report.

You may also want to include the following:

      A. Print Resource Synopsis Sheets
      B. Electronic Resource Synopsis Sheets
      C. Human Resource Synopsis Sheets
      D. Scientific Concept Templates
      E. Vocabulary Word Templates

Scoring the Written Report

Listed below are the criteria that I use to evaluate students who are working on science fair projects under my direction.

Written Report (100 points)

_____ A. Binder (2 points)

_____ B. Cover Page (8 points)
    _____ Title of report (6 points)
        _____ Descriptive (3 points)
        _____ Spelling (3 points)
    _____ Name stated (2 points)

_____ C. Abstract (10 points)
    _____ Good summary (4 points)
    _____ Limited to single paragraph (3 points)
    _____ Spelling (3 points)

_____ D. Table of Contents (10 points)
    _____ Complete (4 points)
    _____ Accurate page numbers (3 points)
    _____ Spelling (3 points)

_____ E. Hypothesis Stated (10 points)
    _____ Stated as a prediction (4 points)
    _____ Original idea (3 points)
    _____ Variable identified (3 points)

_____ F. Background Information (10 points)
    _____ Identified scientific concepts (5 points)
    _____ Identified vocabulary (5 points)

_____ G. Experimental procedure (15 points)
  _____ Materials listed (5 points)
  _____ Procedure (10 points)
      _____ Proper order listed (4 points)
      _____ Safety (3 points)
      _____ Spelling (3 points)

_____ H. Data collected (15 points)
  _____ Data collected properly (10 points)
      _____ Data tables have titles (2 points)
      _____ Data tables have variables and units (3)
      _____ Data plotted accurately (3 points)
      _____ Photos, drawings, notes (2 points)
  _____ Experiment repeated several times (5 points)

_____ I. Conclusions and Findings (15 points)
  _____ Showed relationship to hypothesis (5 points)
  _____ Used data to support hypothesis (5 points)
  _____ Recognize/analyze alternative explanations (5)

_____ J. Appendix (5 points)
  _____ Glossary of terms (2 points)
  _____ Research sheets included (2 points)
  _____ References (1 points)

_____ Total Points   _____ Grade

Display Checklist & Design Ideas

Prepare your display to accompany the report. A good display should include the following:

Freestanding Display

_____ a. freestanding cardboard back
_____ b. title of experiment
_____ c. your name
_____ d. hypothesis
_____ e. findings of the experiment
_____ f. photo or illustrations of equipment
_____ g. data tables or graphs

Additional Display Items

_____ h. a copy of the write-up
_____ i. actual lab equipment setup

Scoring the Display

Listed below are the criteria that I use to evaluate students who are working on science fair projects under my direction.

Display (50 points)

_____ a. freestanding cardboard back (3 points)
_____ b. title of experiment (10 points)
　　_____ descriptive - 5 points
　　_____ centered on board - 2 points
　　_____ spelled correctly - 3 points
_____ c. your name (3 points)
_____ d. hypothesis (4 points)
　　_____ legible - 2 points
　　_____ spelling - 2 points
_____ e. procedure (5 points)
　　_____ list of materials - 2 points
　　_____ directions in logical order - 3 points
_____ f. data tables or graphs (10 points)
　　_____ titles present - 3 points
　　_____ variable and units identified - 3 points
　　_____ clean and well constructed - 4 points
_____ g. findings of the experiment (10 points)
　　_____ data analyzed - 4 points
　　_____ data tied to conclusion - 3 points
　　_____ alternative ideas explored - 3 points
_____ h. additional display items (5 points)
　　_____ a copy of the write-up - 2 points
　　_____ actual lab equipment setup - 3 points

____ Total Points   ____ Grade

Oral Report Checklist

It is entirely possible that you will be asked to make an oral presentation to your classmates. This will give you an opportunity to explain what you did and how you did it. Quite often this presentation is part of your overall score, so if you do well, it will enhance your chances for one of the bigger awards.

To prepare for your oral report, your science fair presentation should include the following components:

Physical Display

_____a. freestanding display board
            hypothesis
            data tables, graphs, photos, etc.
            abstract (short summary)
_____b. actual lab setup (equipment)

Oral Report

_____a. hypothesis or question
_____b. background information
            concepts
            word definitions
            history or scientists
_____c. experimental procedure
_____d. data collected
            data tables
            graphs
            other data
_____e. conclusions and findings
_____f. ask for questions

Set the display board up next to you on the table. Transfer the essential information to index cards, using the outline on the next couple of pages. Use the index cards for reference, but do not read from them. Speak in a clear voice, hold your head up, and make eye contact with your peers. Ask if there are any questions before you finish and sit down. *You should take no fewer than three minutes and no more than 5 minutes to complete your presentation.*

It's Due When ?!? • B. K. Hixson

Card 1 • Introduction

1. Hello. My name is _____
and the title of my project is _____.

Cards 2 & 3 • Hypothesis

2. For my science fair project I was interested in studying
_____ (general topic, like physics) and more specifically I was
curious about _____.
(a specific idea, like polarized light)

3. After some study I chose to isolate a single variable,
_____ (List the variable, like the
amount of water a plant received.) and   proposed the following
hypothesis: _____
_____.
(State your hypothesis.)

Cards 4 & 5 • Background Information

4. In studying my project further I discovered that _____
_____. (List the laws or prin-
ciples, like sound is produced when an object vibrates. Do not get too
involved in regurgitating the laws or ideas. The presentation is about
your work.)

5. The scientist(s) primarily responsible for these discoveries
is/are a man/woman named _____. (List
names.) Give a brief account of who they were and how they discovered the law or idea that they are noted for.

If there are some really interesting facts about that person's life,
you may want to include them, also. (For example, the Nobel physicist, Chien Shung Wu, was originally from China and came to America
to study for a short period of time. While she was here, China was
overthrown by Mao Tse-tung and she never returned to her home-
land.) Cool stuff like that.

Card 6 • Materials

To conduct my experiment I used the following materials:

1. _____
2. _____
3. _____
4. _____ etc.

List and read the materials you used, and include this information πas part of your display, if possible.

Cards 7 & 8 • Experimental Procedure

To conduct my experiment I followed these experimental
procedures:

1. _____
2. _____
3. _____
4. _____ etc.

List and read the procedure you used.

Card 9 & 10 • Data Collected

I collected data in this data table titled : _____.
The variable and its unit was: _____. The constant and its
unit was: _____. (Hold up data table.)

To interpret this data I created a _____ (type) graph.
(Hold up graph.) I repeated the experiment _____ times and this is
reflected in the images that you see.

I also collected photographs/drawings/made notes to accompany the data tables and graphs that I presented. These are representative samples of that work. (Hold up data.)

Card 11 & 12 • Conclusion

My hypothesis was _____. (Restate your hypothesis using Card #2.)

To support my hypothesis the data I have collected should have shown: _____.
(Explain what you were looking for from your data, what you expected to find and why.)

I have concluded that I was a) correct in my assumption or b) incorrect in my assumption. *(Sorry, you can only pick one of these.)* The reason(s) for reaching this decision are _____.
(List the findings of your data and the correlation you drew from each of these findings.)

Thank you for your time. Are there any questions that I can answer?

Scoring the Oral Report

Listed below are the criteria that I use to evaluate students who are working on science fair projects under my direction.

Physical Presence of Speaker (20 points)

_____a. Posture (4 points)
    ____ Speaker facing audience (2 points)
    ____ Speaker exhibits good posture (2 points)

_____b. Appearance (4 points)
    ____ Wearing clean, pressed clothing (2 points)
    ____ Hair clean, combed (2 points)

_____c. Composure (6 points)
    ____ Presentation even and smooth (2 point)
    ____ Speaker smiles, relaxed (2 points)
    ____ Makes regular eye contact (2 points)

_____d. Voice (6 points)
    ____ Appropriate volume for room (3 points)
    ____ Words enunciated properly (3 points)

_____ Subtotal

Oral Report (80 points)

_____a. Introduction (4 points)
    ____ Name stated (2 points)
    ____ Title of report (2 points)

_____b. Subject orientation (12 points)
    ____ Area of science introduced (2 points)
    ____ Topic introduced (2 points)
    ____ Hypothesis stated (4 points)
        ____ Stated as prediction (2 points)
        ____ Original idea (2 points)
    ____ Variable identified (4 points)

_____c. Background information (10 points)
　　　____ Related concepts (5 points)
　　　____ History or scientists (5 points)

_____d. Experimental procedure (15 points)
　　　____ Identified equipment (5 points)
　　　____ Recited procedure (10 points)
　　　　　_____ Proper order listed (7 points)
　　　　　_____ Safety measures described (3 points)

_____e. Data collected (15 points)
　　　____ Data collected properly (8 points)
　　　　　_____ Data tables have variables and units (4)
　　　　　_____ Photos, drawings are accurate, labeled(2)
　　　　　_____ Notes thorough (2)
　　　____ Experiment repeated several times (5 points)
　　　____ Photos or drawings (2 points)

_____f. Conclusions and findings (20 points)
　　　____ Showed relationship to hypothesis (5 pts)
　　　____ Used data to support/refute hypothesis (5 pts)
　　　―― Recognized alternative explanations (5 points)
　　　____ Used data to make predictions (5 points)

_____g. Closing (4 points)
　　　____ Ask for questions (2 points)
　　　____ Thank you (2 points)

_____ Subtotal, Oral Report
_____ Subtotal, Physical Presence

___ Total Points　　　___ Grade

Unfinished Symphony

A German survey party, given the unpleasant task of plotting a road through a centuries-old cemetery, was gingerly picking its way through the tombstones. Suddenly one of the members of the party noticed a very old, chipped, vine-covered monument with faded stonework reading, "L. van Beethoven."

Overcome with curiosity, they decided to open the grave site and see if it was really the master himself that was buried there. As they unearthed the casket, they suddenly stopped when one of the men heard a faint scratching sound coming from inside.

After some discussion they decided to proceed, carefully opening the top of the casket. Much to their collective amazement it was the great composer himself, Ludvig van Beethoven, furiously erasing a score he had begun.

Words finally came to one of the astonished workers and he asked Ludvig what he was doing. Somewhat annoyed, he looked up and replied, "What does it look like I'm doing? I'm decomposing."

This is only the start. Hopefully, you will have several opportunities to ponder, prepare, and present a science fair project. And the next one will always be better.

Answers to Random Brain Splort

Brain Tickler # 1

Review the following sequence of letters. Your task is to cross out *six letters* so that the remaining letters, keeping the sequence exactly the same, spells a very common word.

B S A I N X L E A T N T E A R S

Answer: Sometimes it helps to take things literally. If you cross out SIX LETTERS, the way that it is spelled, rather than six letters, one through six, your answer is quite obvious. Banana.

B S A I N ~~X L E A~~ T N ~~T E A~~ R S

Brain Tickler # 2

Pictured below is a pattern of nine dots arranged in a symmetrical pattern. Connect all of the dots using no more than four straight lines. The only rules are that you may not rearrange the dots and you may not lift your pen or pencil off the page. Good luck.

Do not create artificial boundaries when you are solving problems. Ask ridiculous questions, be obnoxious, have fun, go out of bounds and come back in.

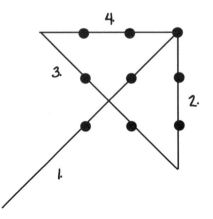

Index

Index